ANCIENT CIVILIZATIONS
Ancient Romans

by Anita Ganeri

COMPASS POINT BOOKS MINNEAPOLIS, MINNESOTA

First American edition published in 2006 by
Compass Point Books
3109 West 50th St., #115
Minneapolis, MN 55410

ANCIENT ROMANS
was produced by
David West Children's Books
7 Princeton Court
55 Felsham Road
London SW15 1AZ

Illustrator: Chris Forsey
Designer: David West
Editors: Kate Newport, Nick Healy
Page Production: Bobbie Nuytten
Content Adviser: Brian S. Hook,
  Assistant Professor, Classics Department,
  University of North Carolina Asheville

Visit Compass Point Books on the Internet at
www.compasspointbooks.com
or e-mail your request to
custserv@compasspointbooks.com

Library of Congress Cataloging-in-Publication Data
Ganeri, Anita, 1961-
  Ancient Romans / by Anita Ganeri.
      p. cm.—(Ancient civilizations)
  Includes bibliographical references and index.
  ISBN 0-7565-1644-7 (hardcover)
  1. Rome—Civilization—Juvenile literature. I. Title. II. Ancient civilizations (Minneapolis, Minn.)
  DG77.G348 2005
  937—dc22   2005025055

  ISBN 0-7565-1759-1 (paperback)

Contents

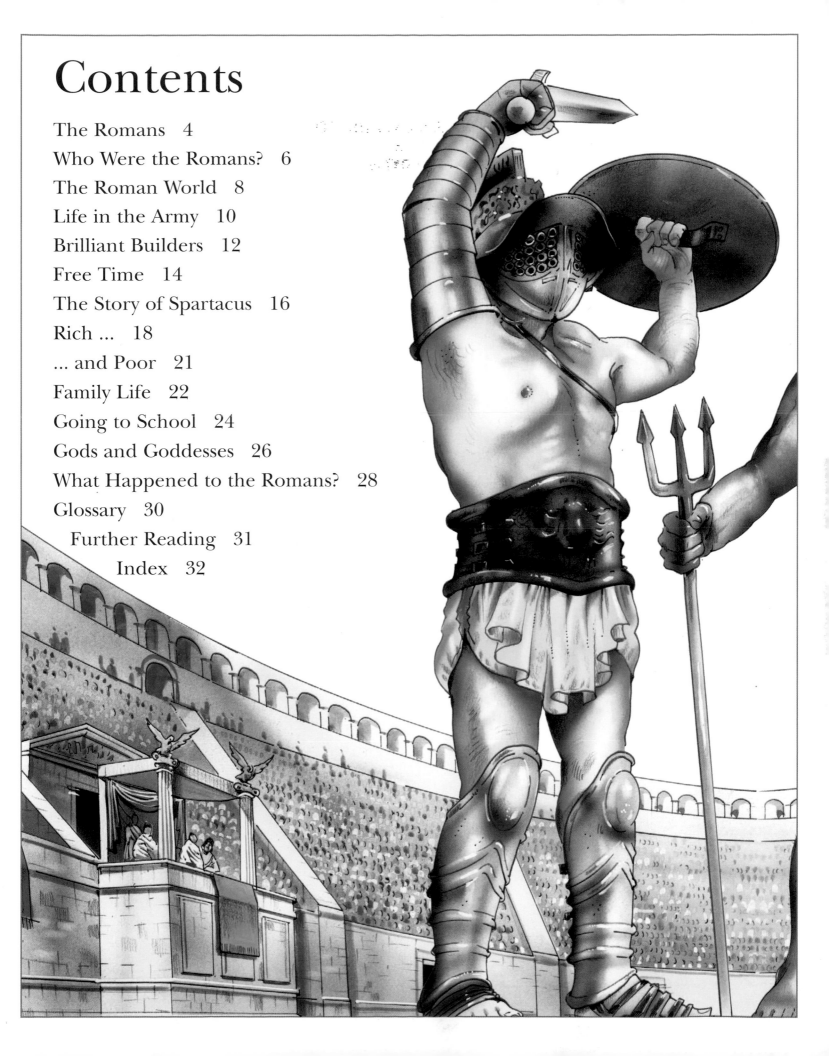

The Romans

Over a period of 1,000 years, ancient Romans built one of the greatest empires the world has ever seen. At its height, nearly 2,000 years ago, the Roman Empire covered an area that is now more than 30 countries, from Britain in the north to modern-day Syria in the east.

Look for this man digging up interesting items from the past, like these Roman coins.

The Romans built great cities and road systems all over their empire and conquered many foreign lands. Although the Romans lived many years ago, we know a lot about their lives.

Who Were the Romans?

The Romans were the people who first lived in Rome, the city in the center of Italy. Later, Romans lived in all parts of their empire. Rome began as a group of small villages built on seven hills next to the Tiber River.

The villages soon grew rich through selling goods to other towns and joined together to form one big city.

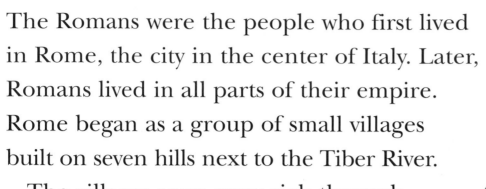
A clay model was dug up from an early Roman tomb. It shows what the village huts may have looked like and tells us something about how ordinary people lived.

The first kings of Rome were Etruscans, the people who lived just north of the Romans in Italy. They were great traders, builders, and soldiers.

At first Rome sometimes had to fight its neighbors. More often, Rome was peaceful. As they grew more powerful, Romans began to take over other cities.

Early Rome was ruled by kings. But in 509 B.C., about 2,500 years ago, the last king was driven out and Rome became a republic. A republic is a place that is ruled by leaders that are chosen by the people.

Legend says that Rome was built by Romulus, the son of Mars, the god of war. Romulus and his twin brother, Remus, were left to die by the Tiber River, but they were found and raised by a she-wolf. The city was built on the spot where they were found.

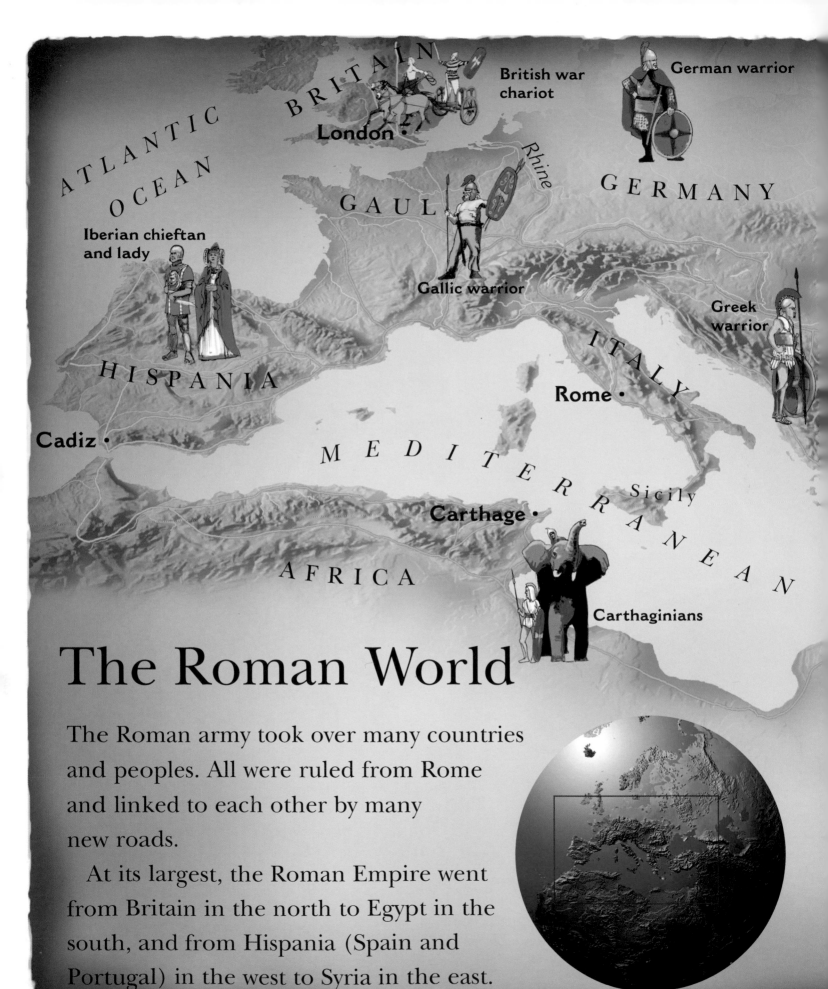

ATLANTIC
OCEAN

BRITAIN

London •

British war
chariot

German warrior

Rhine

GERMANY

Iberian chieftan
and lady

GAUL

Gallic warrior

Greek
warrior

HISPANIA

ITALY

Rome •

Cadiz •

MEDITERRANEAN

Sicily

Carthage •

AFRICA

Carthaginians

The Roman World

The Roman army took over many countries
and peoples. All were ruled from Rome
and linked to each other by many
new roads.

At its largest, the Roman Empire went
from Britain in the north to Egypt in the
south, and from Hispania (Spain and
Portugal) in the west to Syria in the east.

Many coins have been found, stamped with the heads of the Roman emperors. Coins were used for buying and selling and were also made to mark key events, such as great battles.

Augustus

Nero

Hadrian

Dacian warrior

Danube

BLACK SEA

• Byzantium

ANATOLIA

SYRIA

GREECE

• Athens

SEA

JUDEA

Jerusalem

Judean warrior

Alexandria •

EGYPT

Nile

Egyptian war chariot

The main roads linking all parts of the empire are shown in gray. The Roman Empire was at its biggest during the rule of the Emperor Trajan, who died in 117 A.D.

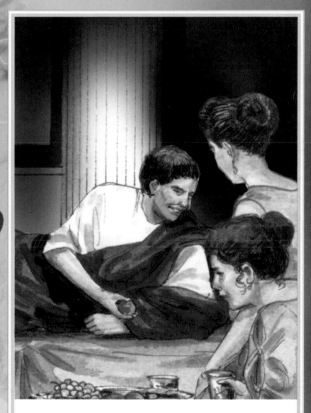

The emperor and certain generals were the only Romans allowed to wear purple togas. This was because purple was the most expensive dye, made from a type of rare seashell.

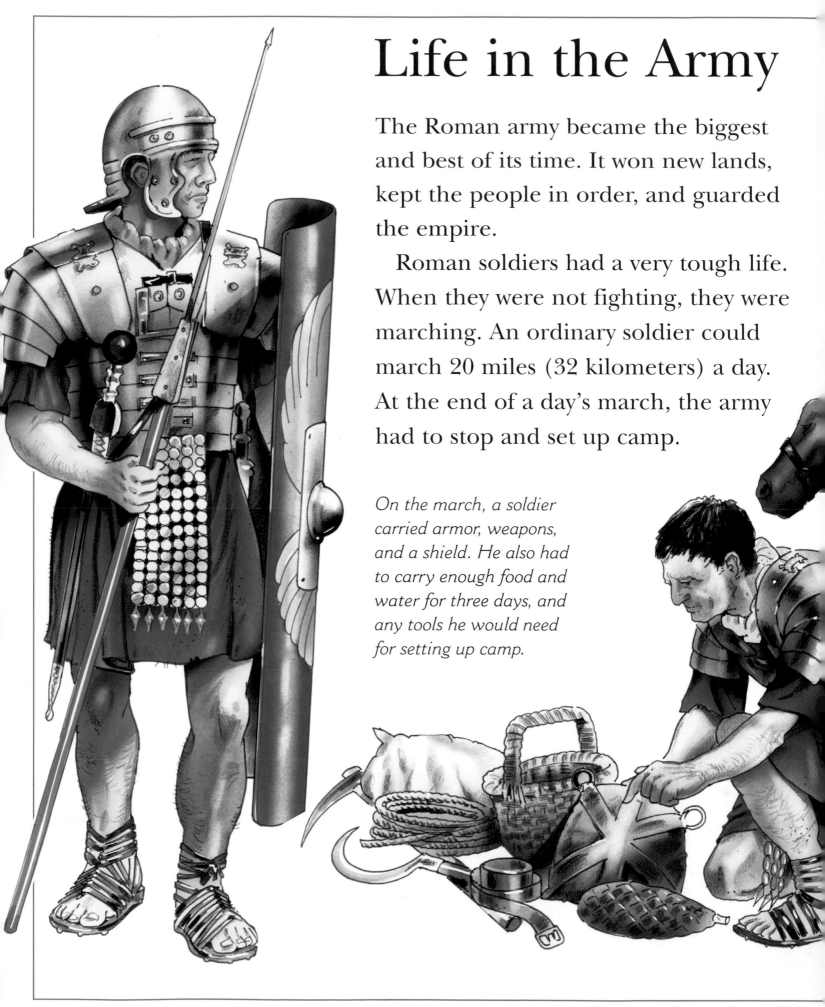

Life in the Army

The Roman army became the biggest and best of its time. It won new lands, kept the people in order, and guarded the empire.

Roman soldiers had a very tough life. When they were not fighting, they were marching. An ordinary soldier could march 20 miles (32 kilometers) a day. At the end of a day's march, the army had to stop and set up camp.

On the march, a soldier carried armor, weapons, and a shield. He also had to carry enough food and water for three days, and any tools he would need for setting up camp.

Eight men shared a mule, which carried a tent and wooden poles.

As protection in battle, soldiers held their shields above their heads and around their bodies for cover. This was called the tortoise, and soldiers hid safely inside.

Soldiers also had to build roads, bridges, and forts. After 25 years, they could retire with a pension or a small area of land to farm.

A soldier's sandals had to be long-lasting. Sandals were made from tough leather with iron studs banged into the soles.

Brilliant Builders

The Colosseum in Rome was completed in 80 A.D. Thousands of Romans could attend a variety of events there.

Engineer

Slaves

The Romans were very good builders. Roman engineers designed—and slaves built—bridges and amphitheaters, such as the Colosseum in Rome. Some Roman aqueducts are still standing today.

The Romans were the first to use concrete and arches, which allowed them to build very large buildings. The emperor paid for the grandest buildings to show how powerful he was.

Roman roads went across the whole empire, stretching for a total of about 53,000 miles (84,800 km). They were mainly used for moving the army and supplies from place to place.

Roads followed the shortest, straightest route between two places. First, a ditch was dug and filled with sand and rubble. Then, flat stone slabs were laid over the rubble. To avoid having puddles, the road was curved, and ditches were used to drain water away.

Giant cranes were used to lift huge stone blocks. They were powered by slaves who walked inside a big wheel.

Road

Aqueduct

Free Time

Samnite

During their holidays, the Romans liked to watch public games, or shows, called ludi. They were paid for by the emperor or wealthy families.

There were three main types of show: wild beast and gladiator fights, chariot races, and theater plays. They were all very popular.

Thousands of people went to the circus, or racetrack, to watch the chariot racing and cheer on their teams—the Blues, Reds, Greens, or Whites. Huge amounts of money were bet on these fast and furious races.

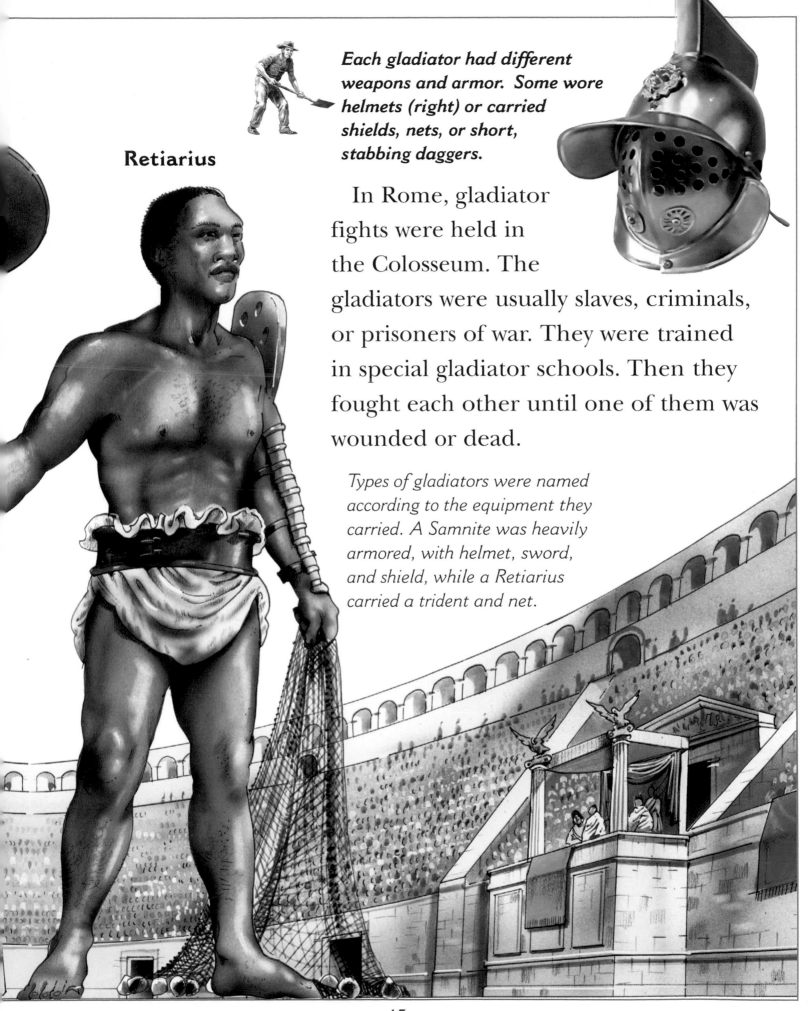

Retiarius

Each gladiator had different weapons and armor. Some wore helmets (right) or carried shields, nets, or short, stabbing daggers.

In Rome, gladiator fights were held in the Colosseum. The gladiators were usually slaves, criminals, or prisoners of war. They were trained in special gladiator schools. Then they fought each other until one of them was wounded or dead.

Types of gladiators were named according to the equipment they carried. A Samnite was heavily armored, with helmet, sword, and shield, while a Retiarius carried a trident and net.

The Story of Spartacus

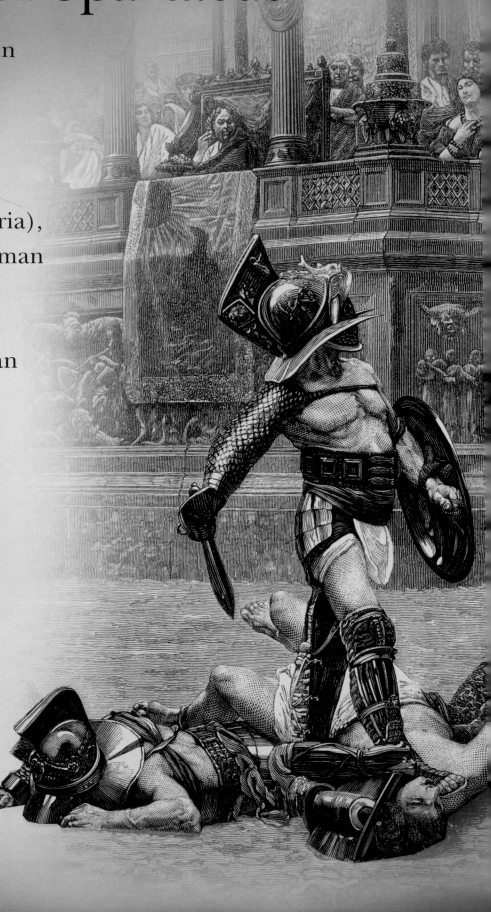

About 2,000 years ago, in 73 B.C., a gladiator slave called Spartacus led a daring rebellion against his Roman masters.

Born in Thrace (Bulgaria), Spartacus had been a Roman soldier before being sold as a slave. His master was Lentulus Batiatus, who ran a school for gladiators in Capua, in southern Italy. At the school, 200 gladiators spent hours each day being taught how to fight and kill. It was very strict. Anyone caught breaking the rules was put into prison.

Spartacus began to form a plan. One night, he led a group of 80 gladiators out of the school, armed only with kitchen tools.

Escaping a fire in the kitchens, Spartacus and the rebels leapt into the street. The alarm was raised right away and guards were sent to find them. But outside, the gladiators found wagons full of weapons and easily fought off the guards. Then they headed out into the countryside and safety.

Every day, their numbers grew as more runaway slaves joined them. For two years, Spartacus and his slave army fought off the Roman army sent to find them, and they killed many Roman soldiers.

The rebels were finally beaten by Crassus and Pompey, two of Rome's leading generals. Thousands of the slaves were caught and crucified, but Spartacus' body was never found. After this, other groups of gladiators tried to rebel. But the Romans were ready and quickly put them down.

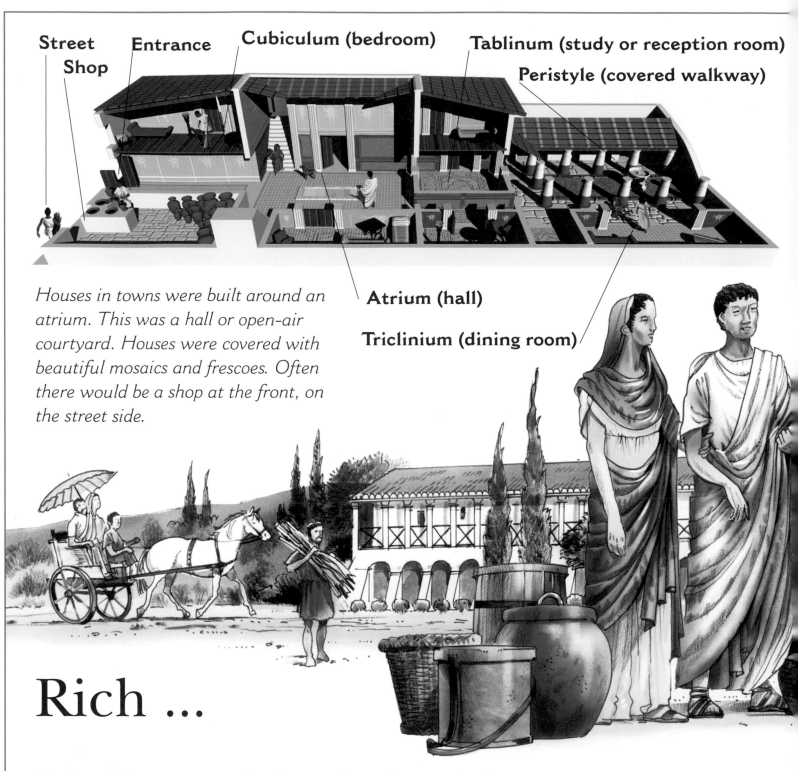

Street Shop Entrance Cubiculum (bedroom) Tablinum (study or reception room)

Peristyle (covered walkway)

Houses in towns were built around an atrium. This was a hall or open-air courtyard. Houses were covered with beautiful mosaics and frescoes. Often there would be a shop at the front, on the street side.

Atrium (hall)

Triclinium (dining room)

Rich ...

Rich and poor people in ancient Rome led very different lives.

Rich Romans often had a town house called a domus, and a country house called a villa. A family visited its villa in the summer to escape from the heat and crowds of Rome.

Wealthy Romans lived very relaxed lives. While they enjoyed themselves, slaves did all the cooking and cleaning. Slaves were often prisoners of war.

Rich Romans gave dinner parties where their guests lay on couches around a large table. Sometimes meals could last for hours and menus included stuffed dormouse or lark and spicy flamingo. Slaves cooked and served the food and looked after the guests.

Most country estates were made up of a large, grand villa and land for growing food. Romans liked to grow olives for making oil and grapes for making wine.

When the family was back in town, the estate was run by a manager and a team of slaves.

Roman slaves had to wear tags with their masters' names written on them and a message saying "Keep me from getting away and return me to my master."

TENEMENE
FVGIAETREVO
CAMEADDOMNV
EVVIVENTIVMI
ARACALLISTI

... and Poor

In Rome and other cities, life was much harder for the poor. They lived in cramped blocks of apartments called insulae. There were often shops and taverns on the ground floor.

The higher up you lived, the smaller your apartment was likely to be. The lower floors were for people who could pay more for the rent.

The apartments had no running water, so people had to get water from the many public fountains in the streets. The only form of heating was wood-burning stoves. They were a big fire hazard and many insulae burned down.

Most apartments did not have a kitchen. Instead, people bought hot food from stalls or snack bars in the streets. A stone carving shows a butcher's shop where richer Romans bought meat.

The narrow city streets of Rome were noisy, crowded, and dirty. People on the top floors simply threw garbage into the street.

After a hard morning's work, many Romans set off for the public baths. Here they bathed in hot and cold pools, then exercised in the gymnasium. The baths were also great places for meeting up with friends.

Family Life

Family life was very important to the Romans. The father was head of the family and was in charge of everyone in the household, including his wife, children, and any slaves he might own.

A nobleman might also give money and advice to people from poorer families. This was in return for their vote in the Senate.

His wife ran the household and looked after the children until they were old enough to go to work or school.

Knucklebones and dice were games played by both upper-class and poor people. Like dice games today, people often gambled on who would win.

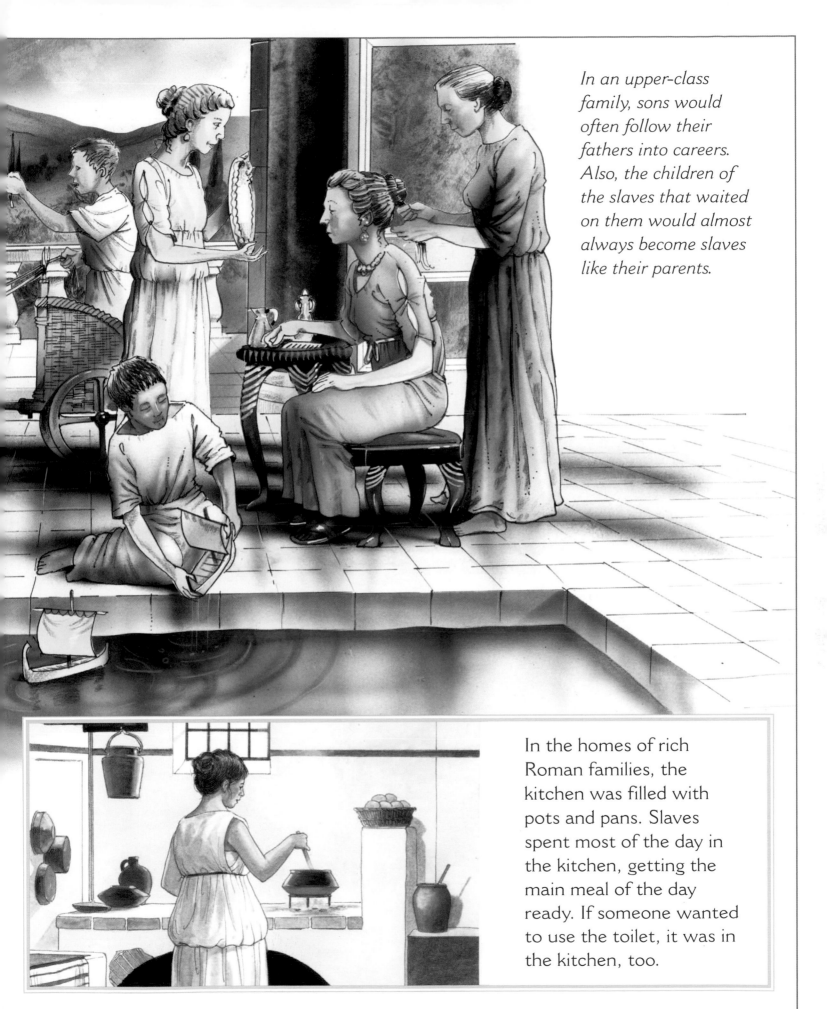

In an upper-class family, sons would often follow their fathers into careers. Also, the children of the slaves that waited on them would almost always become slaves like their parents.

In the homes of rich Roman families, the kitchen was filled with pots and pans. Slaves spent most of the day in the kitchen, getting the main meal of the day ready. If someone wanted to use the toilet, it was in the kitchen, too.

23

Going to School

Roman children from poor families did not go to school. They had to go out to work instead.

Boys with rich parents started school when they were 6 or 7 years old.

Most Roman girls stayed at home with their mothers, who taught them how to run the house and got them ready for marriage.

Children learned to write the Latin alphabet by scratching letters on wooden boards that were covered with wax.

The school day lasted from dawn to about midday. Children learned how to read and write in Latin and Greek, and to do math using Roman numerals.

Older students also had to study and learn the works of famous writers by heart.

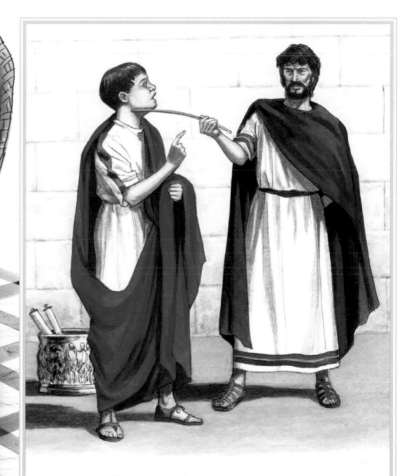

All boys from noble families had to learn how to speak in public. They went to a special teacher called a rhetor. Training began when boys were 13 or 14 years old and took many years.

Gods and Goddesses

The Romans worshipped many different gods and goddesses. Among the main gods were Jupiter, the king of the gods, and Mars, the god of war.

People feared the gods and tried to please them with lots of gifts and sacrifices.

Many Romans believed in magic. A hand model has lots of symbols to help keep evil away.

Romans believed that soothsayers could read the future. The Romans went to see them before starting anything new, like a journey. Soothsayers interpreted the future by looking for signs in the sky and even in the bodies of animals.

If anything went wrong, people said it was because the gods were angry.

Many beautiful temples were built for the gods. Each had a statue of its own god or goddess. People could go inside the temple to say their prayers.

The temple priests also carried out rituals and animal sacrifices to win the gods' favor.

The Romans thought that there were spirits that looked after the household and even protected the storage cupboard. Families prayed to these household gods to look after them. Each home had a small area where the family worshipped every day.

What Happened to the Romans?

About 1,700 years ago, the Roman Empire began to face problems. People were unhappy with rising prices and taxes, and the rulers were finding it hard to hold onto power.

Barbarian tribes began to invade, and the weakened Roman army could not control their lands anymore.

The Huns from eastern Asia took over lands of other tribes and pushed them west into the Roman Empire.

We still copy the look of ancient Rome when building houses and towns today.

The empire was split into east and west by Emperor Diocletian in 284 A.D. But 200 years later, Rome was taken over by a tribe called the Visigoths from Germany. The last western Roman emperor was called Romulus Augustulus.

Emperor Constantine the Great briefly reunited the empire in 324 A.D. and built a new capital city, Constantinople (now Istanbul). He became the first Christian emperor of Rome.

Glossary

amphitheaters—circular, open-air buildings for entertainment such as gladiator fights

aqueducts—covered waterways or channels used to transport fresh water

artifacts—human-made objects found at historical sites

barbarian—the name for people living outside Roman lands

empire—a large state made up of many countries, all ruled by a leader called an emperor

frescoes— large pictures painted on wet plaster

Latin—the language that early Romans spoke

mosaics—patterns made of tiny tiles

pension—money paid regularly to people who have retired from work

rebellion—a fight against a government or ruler

republic—a state or country that is ruled by leaders elected by the people

rituals—sets of actions or prayers carried out by a priest or worshippers

sacrifice—when an animal or living thing is killed to honor the gods

Senate—the group of officials that ruled Rome before the emperor

toga—the loose, flowing robes worn by Roman noblemen on special occasions

trident—a large forklike weapon

Further Resources

AT THE LIBRARY

Blacklock, Dyan. *The Roman Army: The Legendary Soldiers Who Created an Empire*. New York: Walker, 2004

Dubois, Muriel L. *Ancient Rome*. Mankato, Minn.: Capstone Press, 2004.

Lassieur, Allison. *The Ancient Romans*. New York: Franklin Watts, 2004.

ON THE WEB

For more information on *Ancient Romans,* use FactHound
to track down Web sites related to this book.

1. Go to *www.facthound.com*
2. Type in a search word related to this book
   or this book ID: 0756516447
3. Click on the *Fetch It* button.

FactHound will find the best Web sites for you.

LOOK FOR MORE BOOKS IN THIS SERIES

ANCIENT GREEKS
ISBN 0-7565-1646-3

ANCIENT MAYA
ISBN 0-7565-1677-3

THE VIKINGS
ISBN 0-7565-1678-1

Index